*Meet*CINDY SHERMAN

ARTIST • PHOTOGRAPHER • CHAMELEON

JAN GREENBERG
and SANDRA JORDAN

A NEAL PORTER BOOK
ROARING BROOK PRESS
NEW YORK

Untitled #415, 2004

Contents

For all our daughters, girlfriends, and sisters—strong, talented, independent women who continue to surprise and inspire us   —J.G. and S.J.

Text copyright © 2017 by Jan Greenberg and Sandra Jordan
A Neal Porter Book
Published by Roaring Brook Press
Roaring Brook Press is a division of Holtzbrinck Publishing
Holdings Limited Partnership
175 Fifth Avenue, New York, NY 10010
mackids.com

Library of Congress Cataloging-in-Publication Data
Names: Greenberg, Jan, 1942– author. | Jordan, Sandra
    (Sandra Jane Fairfax), author.
Title: Meet Cindy Sherman : artist, photographer, chameleon
    / by Jan Greenberg & Sandra Jordan.
Description: New York : Roaring Brook Press, 2017 | "A Neal Porter
    Book." | Audience: Ages 7–12 | Includes bibliographical
    references.
Identifiers: LCCN 2016058238 | ISBN 9781626725201 (hardcover)
Subjects: LCSH: Sherman, Cindy—Juvenile literature. | Photographers—
    Biography—Juvenile Literature. | Photography, Artistic—Juvenile literature.
Classification: LCC TR140.S5187 G74 2017 | DDC 770.92 [B]—dc23
LC record available at https://lccn.loc.gov/2016058238

Our books may be purchased in bulk for promotional,
educational, or business use. Please contact your local
bookseller or the Macmillan Corporate and Premium Sales
Department at (800) 221-7945 ext. 5442 or by e-mail at
MacmillanSpecialMarkets@macmillan.com.

First edition, 2017
Book design by Dirk Kaufman
Printed in China by Toppan Leefung Printing Ltd.,
Dongguan City, Guangdong Province

10 9 8 7 6 5 4 3 2 1

A NOTE TO OUR READERS

Art is for everyone at every age. We asked some young friends to share their thoughts about Cindy Sherman's artwork. Scattered throughout this book, you will read their responses. "What do you see?" we asked. "Who is the person in this photograph?" "What is happening here?" Our viewers didn't always agree with each other, or with us, but that's okay. There are no right or wrong answers. We invite you to enter Cindy's invented but somehow familiar world and discover your own stories.

Jan and Sandra

Untitled Film Still #13, 1978

Meet Cindy Sherman

In a tranquil suburb of Long Island, New York, there once lived a girl who didn't want to be

 a princess,

 a movie star,

 a ballerina,

 or a prom queen.

Yet she did love playing dress-up and pretending to be someone else.

She put tape on her face and pulled it into strange shapes to look like a ghoul.

She painted herself with poster paint and took the train into New York City with her friends to spend an afternoon "fake" shopping as the paint peeled off her eyelids.

"I would make myself up as a monster," Cindy says, "... which seemed like much more fun than just looking like Barbie."

In the basement closet she found her great-grandmother's old-fashioned dress and bloomers and disguised herself as an old lady, complete with slumped shoulders, sagging bosom, and

Snapshot of Cindy (on left) and friend Janet, c. 1966

Banner from the Museum of Modern Art's exhibit of Cindy Sherman's artwork, 2012

spectacles. Cindy and her friend Janet sucked their lips over their teeth to appear toothless and walked up and down the street "trying to trick the neighbors."

People thought she was just a kid, pretending, fooling around. After all, they said, that's what kids do before they grow up.

But when Cindy did grow up, her same fooling around with cosmetics and costumes triggered a revolution in art making and caused the world to look at photography in a new way. How did Cindy Sherman, a seemingly ordinary American girl from an ordinary American background, become an international art star and an inspiration to a whole generation of young artists? Photographs of Cindy have appeared in museums and magazines, on the Internet, and even on the side of a building in New York City. Yet if you saw her walking down the street, you wouldn't recognize her. How has she managed to hide in plain sight?

Who is Cindy Sherman?

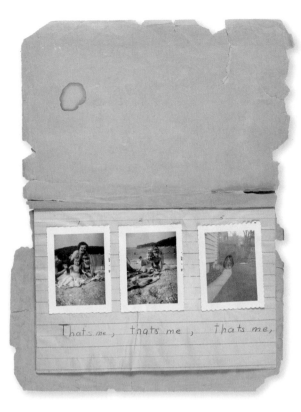

Thats me, thats me, Thats me,

That's me, That's me,

Thats me, Thats me,

Thats me, Tha's me,

Thats me,

That's me That's me,

Thats me, Thats me,

Pages from "A Cindy Book," 1964–75

Chapter 1

Where It All Began

"There were no sidewalks, it was a small community. I went barefoot all summer long and would just put on my bathing suit, take a towel and walk or bike to the beach."

Cindy received a small, easy-to-use Kodak Brownie camera for her tenth birthday. She started snapping pictures of her friends and family and pasted the photographs into a homemade scrapbook along with pictures of herself.

She called it "A Cindy Book" and circled her face, with "That's me" scribbled under every photo. "I added to it periodically as a preteen." Ten years later, home from college, she rediscovered the half-finished album and revised it into an art piece.

Still from I Love Lucy *TV show*   *Interior of a thrift store*

"I was the youngest of five children . . . There were nineteen years between me and my oldest sibling, so my family had been together a long time before I came into the picture. I was trying to find my way and to belong." The scrapbook came out of that longing.

In the background of some of the photos are glimpses of her hometown, Huntington. Her parents had moved there in 1955, the year after Cindy was born. Although bustling New York City was little more than an hour away, the quiet Long Island suburb could not have been more different. Cindy bicycled around by herself without her parents worrying about where she was or what she was up to.

"The beach was rocky, not sandy . . . I fished from the dock near where my father kept our sailboat. There was a pavilion at the beach which occasionally held dance parties."

If she wasn't biking or directing her friends and young relatives in make-believe games, Cindy could be found in front of the television. There were just three channels available; sitcoms, movies, and cartoons played endlessly.

On these programs women generally took supporting roles as mothers, wives, or sidekicks to the hero. TV moms wore skirts, not slacks, even when they bustled about the kitchen cooking dinner. Their hair was sprayed to perfection, makeup perfectly applied.

"I was always the kid watching TV and doing something else," says Cindy.

At the same time, she kept busy, cutting and pasting pictures, gluing together felt clothes for her troll doll, and drawing paper dolls. Later, as a teenager, she designed miniature paper copies of all her clothes so she could plan her outfits for school.

Cindy says, "I'd put on makeup every day of the year because I thought, 'Well, you never know who's going to knock on the door.'"

For Cindy, TV and her art activities were more interesting than books. Her mother, who taught reading to children with learning problems, didn't fuss at Cindy for not being a reader. Mrs. Sherman understood her daughter's artistic spirit, her need to make things.

From time to time she drove Cindy to the Salvation Army store so she could gather cast-off clothes for a special costume trunk she filled with old prom dresses. Cindy's father, who collected cameras, enjoyed taking photographs and shooting home movies of the family.

Making art came naturally to Cindy, though she doesn't remember her parents taking her to museums or art galleries. When she was accepted to college, she chose to major in art but didn't know what artists actually did.

"My idea of being an artist as a kid was a courtroom artist or one of those boardwalk artists who do caricatures," says Cindy.

Her parents approved of her decision, yet her mother suggested that Cindy take some education classes so she could teach to support herself.

"We didn't know that any artists made money," says Cindy.

This artwork was painted by the teenaged Cindy Sherman. "When I was in high school, I was more into painting than photography," says Cindy. "Obviously, I must've been influenced by Easy Rider, *and that was probably my vision of the ideal boyfriend that I dreamed of having. I think I was just copying styles of the era, trying to make something 'cool,' or shall we say 'groovy.'"*

Chapter 2
College Days

"I always felt like an artist, though I had no idea what it meant to be an artist."

Eighteen-year-old Cindy packed her bags and went off to the State University of New York at Buffalo (known as Buff State). Her parents packed their bags, too, and sold the family house on Long Island. They moved to a retirement community in New Jersey. Cindy had a bedroom there with her old furniture, but her friendships and the familiar neighborhood where she had grown up were left behind.

She says, "Home was not home. I was coming to a village of old people."

Cindy knew it was time to grow up. Her fellow art students became her second family.

Like all the art majors, Cindy plunged into the typical required courses: painting , sculpture, and photography.

Photography was a problem for her. The teacher concentrated on the dry, technical aspects of the picture-making process. There were no digital cameras. Automatic cameras existed, but students were not allowed to use them.

Instead, they loaded black-and-white film into their cameras and measured available light with a handheld meter. They learned how to adjust the camera's focus and speed before taking a picture. They mixed chemicals for developing film in the darkroom.

Cindy says, "None of that made any sense to me."

She flunked the course and had to take it over.

Untitled, 1975: Twenty-three black-and-white photographs in an accordion booklet, hand-colored

Fortunately, the next year she had a new teacher, Barbara Jo Revelle, who said a photographer's ideas mattered more than technique. Freed from the demand for perfect negatives and prints, Cindy experimented. Revelle called her work "strangely dazzling, risky."

Cindy was good at drawing and painting. She could copy anything, but painting bored her. With a camera Cindy found she had a lot to say. Not everyone at Buff State was thrilled with her new direction. When she changed her major from painting to photography, her adviser accused her of "not being serious."

"I was demoted from a bachelor of fine arts degree to just a bachelor of arts," she says.

Times had changed as well. In the 1970s a liberated woman "did not wear makeup. You did not dye your hair, you didn't wear a bra—we were all natural," says Cindy. But she still spent hours experimenting with beauty products and putting outfits together.

Imagine Cindy, surrounded by all those secondhand clothes, jars of makeup, tubes of lipstick, and wigs, turning the camera on herself. She became her own model. In a set of twenty-three photographs, a plain, frumpy girl in horn-rimmed glasses—"which was how I looked"—was transformed into a girl who might shock her parents. This was Cindy's take on the "beauty

Ashford Hollow Foundation, Essex Arts Center, where the exhibition space Hallwalls was started

makeover" familiar to any reader of the glossy magazines aimed at girls and women. The piece, which she refers to as her "first artwork," was exhibited in a group show at the Albright-Knox Art Gallery, Buffalo's world-famous art museum.

At Buff State, Cindy, her boyfriend, the artist Robert Longo, and other student friends lived in the loft space of a warehouse that had been renovated into artists' housing. They turned the hallways of the old building into an art gallery, calling it simply Hallwalls. Cindy helped paint walls and mount art shows.

Sometimes for Hallwalls' art openings, Cindy showed up masquerading as a character— a pregnant woman or the TV star Lucille Ball. With her growing collection of costumes, she role-played, disguising herself in front of the big mirror in her studio. This was Cindy's way of escaping to a make-believe world when she felt blue or bored. "Sometimes," she says, "I was inspired by an item of clothing."

Untitled (Lucy), 1975/2001.
Cindy dresses up as Lucille Ball

Untitled stills from Doll Clothes, *1975*

Paper dolls had appealed to Cindy ever since she was a kid back in Huntington. Now she made a short animated film entitled *Doll Clothes*. It tells the story of a cutout paper doll—Cindy—who comes to life. She tries on, then takes off, one getup after another. Unhappy with all of them, the disappointed paper doll ends up back in her underwear.

Cindy also created a series of collage storyboards that spread out across a wall. She photographed herself in various poses, costumed like a fairy in a mini-dress with wings on her back.

By the time she graduated in 1976, her portfolio was filled with art projects. She didn't know where she would live or how she would support herself, but she'd already found the central focus of her life's work. "I decided to use the camera as a means of exploring my experiences as a woman."

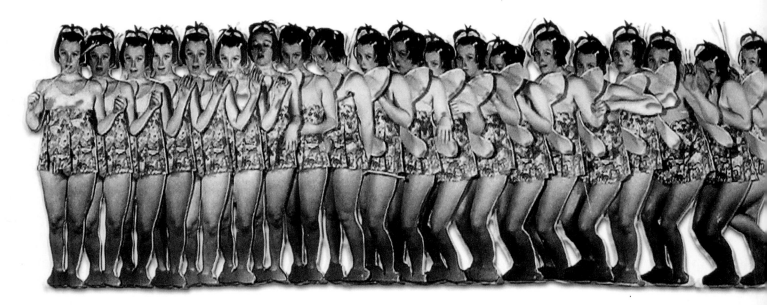

Scale Relationship Series (Version II), 1976, 37 black-and-white cutout photographs

She stayed in Buffalo, where she had friends and a studio to make art. Her work appeared in several group exhibitions. Reviewers in newspapers singled her out.

Then fate gave her a push. She won a $3,000 grant from the National Endowment for the Arts. Robert Longo said, "You've got the money. Let's go."

They threw their things in his van and moved to New York City.

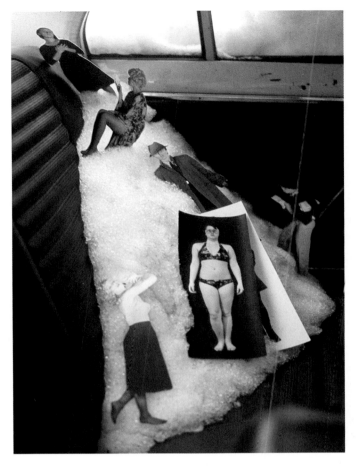

Snow Show was a spur-of-the-moment Hallwalls show in 1977 that celebrated a big Buffalo blizzard. Here's an installation of Cindy's photographic cutouts in the backseat of her car

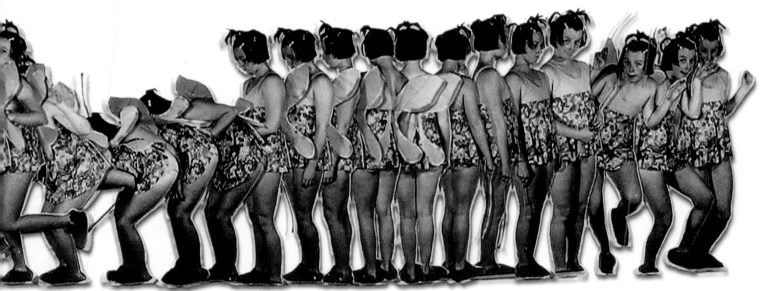

Chapter 3

New York, New York

"I didn't think I was actually going to make a difference. We all would have been happy just to have a show somewhere."

New York City intimidated Cindy—dirty, dangerous, and crowded. For the first few months, she barely left the small apartment she and Robert rented on Fulton Street in lower Manhattan, but she couldn't hide out forever. To pay for film, as well as rent and food, she ventured out to hunt for a job.

Helene Winer, the director of the gallery Artists Space, recognized her talent. Cindy had shown her series *Murder Mystery* in a show at the gallery with other Buffalo artists. Helene said, "I liked her and she needed a job." Cindy started there as a part-time receptionist.

There was a relaxed, easygoing atmosphere at Artists Space. Cindy came to work one day dressed as a secretary in a wig and glasses. Another time she appeared as a nurse, complete with cap and uniform.

"I'd be home fooling around with makeup and a costume . . . and suddenly I'd look at my watch and go, 'Oh, wow, I have to get to work. Well. O.K., I'll just go like this.'"

One evening she and Robert visited the studio of an artist whose day job was at a company that published sleazy magazines and paperbacks. In a corner she found a stack of photographs that had been used for their various publications. They reminded Cindy of black-and-white film stills, shots of actors used to promote movies in the media.

"If you look at one, you make up your own story," she says.

Back in Buffalo she'd already photographed herself as different characters. Now she had an inspiration. She could imitate these film stills but not base her photos on real movies.

"I wanted them to seem cheap and trashy, something you'd find in a novelty store and buy for a quarter. I didn't want them to look like art."

She purposely developed the film so that the photographs would look cracked and grainy. As she applied makeup and tried on her

Fulton Street, downtown New York City

Untitled (Secretary), 1978/1993

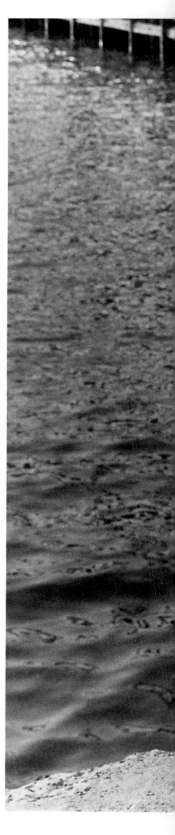

collection of thrift shop wigs and castoffs, a character would come to mind. She found herself acting out all the clichéd roles that young women played in Hollywood films—

a housewife, a working girl, a glamour girl, a small-town tourist in a big city.

"I took a couple of photos here and there, in the bathroom, in the hallway," Cindy says. "I made lists of characters missing to diversify the group."

Robert drove Cindy around downtown New York looking for other locations. She didn't want anyone in the background of the photograph. When she found a spot that looked interesting, Robert stopped the van and waited while Cindy hopped in back to change. She emerged completely disguised. A dark wig covered her hair. Heavy eyebrows and eyeliner sloped toward her temples. Robert climbed on top of the van to get the angle Cindy wanted. While she directed him, he snapped several pictures. Robert said, "She looked pretty weird sometimes."

During a visit with her parents, who had moved to Arizona, Cindy brought along an empty suitcase to shop for clothes at a Salvation Army store, just in case there might be a photo opportunity. She had her chance during a family road trip.

Murder Mystery, 1976, 4 of 255 black-and-white cutout photographs

Untitled Film Still #25, 1978

Untitled Film Still #48, 1979

Lucy (age 11): The scenery looks like the West to me. Maybe she lives on a ranch with horses. She's waiting on the side of the road for one of those buses, you know, the ones in the country that you flag down. Her little suitcase is there. She's not dressed for a date. Maybe she's going to spend the night with a friend or she's running away from home.

On a lonely stretch of highway, she told her father, "Stop here," and climbed into the backseat of the station wagon to change. Once she decided on her outfit and a place to sit, she instructed him to snap what has become one of her best-known pictures. He shot five or six frames, but only the pose in which she stood up and turned her face away conveyed the mood she was after.

Cindy is often surprised by reactions to her photographs. "I like the idea that people who don't know anything about art can appreciate it without having to know the history of photography and painting." She says her work is labeled "Untitled" because she doesn't want to influence the viewer's response.

We, the viewers, are on our own, confronted by these make-believe women who seem all too real.

After four years on the project of photographing herself in many roles, Cindy ended the series at sixty-nine images. Her characters were beginning to repeat themselves, she says. With Untitled Film Stills, she established the basic framework of her practice (her body of work), the rich material she has explored for more than thirty years.

She uses herself as both director and model.

She does all her own makeup, costumes, and lighting.

She suggests or implies a story.

She works in series, groups of photographs related by theme.

She presents stereotypes—common ways society labels women—for example, by their age, attractiveness, clothing, or social status.

She is a chameleon, changing her appearance from photograph to photograph, so that she is many people but never Cindy.

When Untitled Film Stills was exhibited in New York City at the Kitchen, a not-for-profit artist-run gallery, critics and collectors alike took serious notice. Cindy was an immediate sensation. A few years later the Museum of Modern Art would refer to Untitled Film Stills as "a landmark body of work."

Untitled #66, 1980

Coco (age 11): She's on a highway, running away from someone or something. The background is bluish . . . maybe the sun has gone down. Is she lit up from a car's headlights or a flashlight? Someone is looking for her. She's holding on to a handle. Is it a suitcase? A bicycle?

Frankie (age 10): She looks scared. Maybe a police car is behind her. She's looking back, saying, "I'm in big trouble." She's near a small town. There are mountains or hills in the background. She's standing in the road and cars are coming toward her.

Chapter 4

Rear Screen Projections, Centerfolds, Fairy Tales, and More

"When I'm working on my photographs I have to make up my own sort of rules. Sometimes I have a vision of what I want but mostly I'm guided by what I don't want."

Rear Screen Projections 1980–1981

During the time when Cindy was making Untitled Film Stills, she decided she needed her own place. She wanted to work completely alone. Even today, few people have been allowed to watch as she sinks herself into a character. The tiny loft apartment she found had a toilet down the hall, a two-burner hotplate for cooking, and a corner she curtained off to serve as both a closet and a darkroom.

For her next series, Cindy borrowed a high-powered projector. Adapting a technique used in old Hollywood movies, she projected a slide onto a screen and posed in front of it. The color looks faded, like an old snapshot left in a drawer. Introducing color into her pictures allowed Cindy a wider visual variety.

"Black-and-white lends such a nostalgic feeling to photographs and I wanted to move on."

Untitled #96, 1981

Coco: She looks like she might be in college, maybe a teenager. This is a person from twenty years ago. I can tell by what she's wearing.

Frankie: She doesn't look happy, like she's done something wrong. She's confused. Judging from her expression, she's trying to figure out her life.

Centerfolds 1981

After Untitled Film Stills gained so much positive attention both in reviews and by word of mouth, people began seeking her out for projects. *Artforum*, an influential journal, featured a different artist every month in its center pages. When an editor asked Cindy to participate, she hoped for something unusual. What Cindy sent her was both unexpected and disturbing. "It was my idea to do centerfolds," says the artist. But they aren't photographs of a beguiling woman lying across the page of a magazine with few clothes on and a big smile.

In Cindy's version the camera points down at the figure as if someone is looming over her. "I wanted to comment on the nature of centerfolds," Cindy says, "where you see a woman lying there, but in mine you look closer and suddenly realize, 'Oops, I didn't mean to invade this private moment.' I wanted to make people feel uncomfortable."

What was so upsetting to the *Artforum* editor? At a time when the feminist movement was gathering steam, she worried that the women in Cindy's centerfolds looked troubled and vulnerable instead of strong and independent. Would they be viewed as victims? The editor regretfully returned the photographs without publishing them.

A few months later Metro Pictures, a new gallery opened by Helene Winer, showed the same artworks. Blown up to a 24-by-48-inch size, they stretched across the gallery walls in an almost life-size format. Controversial? Yes, to some people. But Cindy Sherman's artwork spoke of the lives of women and the equal rights issues they were marching for and debating. "Even though I've never actively thought of my work as feminist … everything in it was drawn from my observations as a woman in this culture."

In Untitled #96, the lush rust and melon colors of the girl's sweater and plaid skirt are repeated in the color and shapes of the floor. She looks unhappy, lost in thought. In one hand she holds a crumpled page of personal ads from a newspaper. Before online dating, this was one of the ways people met each other.

In Untitled #92, our attention is riveted on the girl's brightly lit face. This is how the artist emphasizes a feeling of menace. The stage is set for our reactions.

Ananya (age 12): She looks like she's stuck in an attic. She looks panicked in a dark, cramped space. Her hair's wet. Was she pushed in there from the rain, because inside the floor is dry? This reminds me of Cinderella when her stepmother locked her up.

Kit (age 12): She might have been getting ready for school. This reminds me of the uniform I used to have to wear every day at school.

Untitled #92, 1981

Madeline (age 13): This girl is about eighteen and has moved away from home. Now she's met somebody and is waiting for him to call. Her hands are clenched. She's tense and giving up hope. The old phone and her nubby pink robe with poofy sleeves show that this is not in super-modern times.

Arianna (age 17): This is definitely happening in the 1980s. My mom told me when she was growing up and waiting for a boy to call, she had to stretch out the phone cord so she could talk in private. The girl is thinking, "Why hasn't he called me?"

Untitled #90, 1981

A tender rosy light gently bathes the arm, shoulder, and cheek of Untitled #90. The young girl's face is in shadow as she stares at the old-fashioned white phone. The subject, cropped and head-on, dominates the frame. Is she longing for the call that hasn't come or dreading it? It could be romance that has grabbed the girl's attention. Perhaps a boyfriend has promised to call. But she also could be waiting for news from her family about a parent in the hospital, a brother in trouble. Cindy is not an actress, but she convinces us that her character is real, even as we imagine these different scenarios.

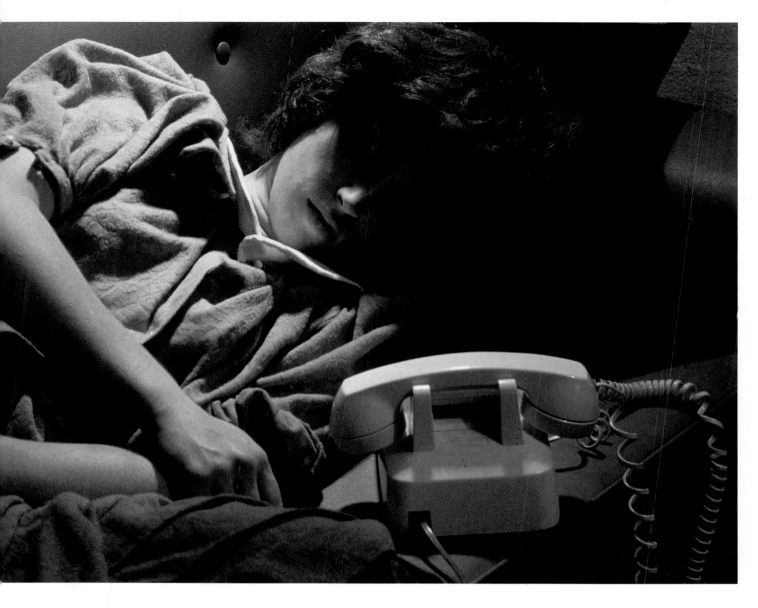

Imagine Cindy alone in her studio, putting on makeup, a wig, and a costume, then setting up the shot for each photo in the series. Wouldn't it be easier to use models? Not really.

Privacy gives Cindy the freedom she needs to work.

Cindy says, "Briefly in the '80s I tried using friends and family and even hired an assistant to pose, and I felt like I just had to entertain them, be conscious of 'Do you need coffee now?' And they'd be kind of giggly because they were being made up to look funny. I push myself, but I don't push other people."

Untitled #122, 1983

Ananya: She looks like someone who is usually perfectly dressed. But she's mad, like someone hurt her badly and now she doesn't care how she looks. Waves of anger radiate off her. She might be saying, "You ruined me and now I'm out to get you."

Kit: She looks like a crazy, psycho dead person, crying blood. Someone hurt her.

Lilliana (age 12): She's at work and did something wrong. She's mad at herself and knows she's getting fired.

Fashion Pictures 1983–1984

Cindy says, "I grew up with my mother telling me I had to be nice and be perceived as nice and generous, but we're not always." People who meet Cindy describe her as a girl's girl, friendly and chatty, happy to talk about men and makeup. But she has another, tougher side, a Cindy Sherman who is not trying to be polite or to please anyone except herself. It comes out in her art.

When the owner of a New York boutique asked her to produce advertisements for a hip magazine, Cindy didn't pose like a typical fashion model—quite the opposite. Her characters projected attitudes ranging from disheveled to deranged.

She says, "I'm disgusted with how people get themselves up to look beautiful. I'm much more fascinated with the other side . . . I was trying to make fun of fashion."

In Untitled #122, the black power suit would fit in any corporate boardroom, but the blonde wearing it has wild, tousled hair and pink makeup to suggest blood in her one visible eye.

Cindy says, "Once I'm set up, the camera starts clicking, then I just start to move in the mirror. It's not like I'm method acting or anything. I don't feel that I am that person. I may be thinking about a certain story or situation, but I don't become her. There's this distance. The image in the mirror becomes her—the image the camera gets on film. And one thing I've always known is that the camera lies."

Untitled #119, 1983

Karl (age 13): She's singing on a stage because there's a spotlight on her. But if she was really well known, there would be more spotlights. If she's not singing, she's yelling.

Gunnar (age 13): She's definitely singing, maybe belting out, "What did you do again?" Her whole outfit is coordinated, even her blue earrings.

Fairy Tales 1985

Up until now, the people in Cindy's pictures remind us of women we might notice browsing in a shop, walking down a city street, or sitting in a restaurant. In her next series, the artist steps away from modern life into fairy tales and fantasy. The subjects are not charming princes and princesses. Cindy's interest does not lie there. Instead she chooses images from the dark side, subjects dealing with violence and the grotesque.

This called for a set of new props, replicas of body parts that she bought in costume or magic stores and later ordered from catalogs: feet, chests, bellies, noses, foreheads, tongues.

Untitled #150, 1985

Jay Shaun (age 11): She's all wet and fingering her tongue. It looks slimy and red. You can tell it's not her real tongue. At first I thought it was a lollipop. She's staring at someone but you can't tell who it is. She must be standing high up because the people behind her on the beach are tiny.

The creature with the big tongue in Untitled #150 doesn't look human. Is it a goblin, an elf, or a gargoyle out of a bad dream?

In Untitled #153 (opposite page), is this a fairy princess waiting for a prince to kiss her back to life? Or is she the wicked witch who has come to a bad end? As always with Cindy's images, there is just a glimpse of a story.

Lexie (age 13): Is this a woman or a man? Could be a prince with the hair curled around the ears in that haircut princes have. He looks dead, but not really. Is he frozen? The color is very cool, silvery. Like moonlight.

Lucy: Is this a he or a she? I think he's not really dead. More like petrified, like the people in the second *Harry Potter*. It's a spell. He might come back to life.

Untitled #153, 1985

Untitled #172, 1987

Karl: This is a messy table. It looks like a watermelon was smashed on the candelabra, but it's really melting wax. The candles have been burning a long time. People at the party might have had an argument and left. There's a dark silhouette of a figure lurking in back. I can see a nose. Whose is it? The food on the plate looks like worms. Maybe that's why everyone left.

Gunnar: It's a disaster. Someone might have dropped a plate and forgotten about it. Whoever set up this meal must be extremely insane.

Disasters 1986–1989

Cindy likes to watch horror movies. She's attracted to material some people might call gross. She says, "It intrigues me why certain things are repulsive. To think about why something repulses me makes it more interesting. I feel that I have to explore it." This artwork, at left, could be a scene at a ghoul's dinner table. The subject matter is startling.

Most of Cindy's photographs include a figure. At first glance there doesn't seem to be one here. Look again.

Isn't art supposed to be beautiful? Can we find beauty in ugliness? The beauty of these almost abstract compositions was lost upon Cindy's fans. Many of them were repelled and confused. They were put off by the props: broken dolls, ghoulish masks, glass eyeballs, trash and debris. Harsh lighting and bizarre colors added to their dismay.

For Cindy, success came with self-doubt. Had her images grown too easy? Pleasing the public was not Cindy's goal. These photographs were intentionally hard to view.

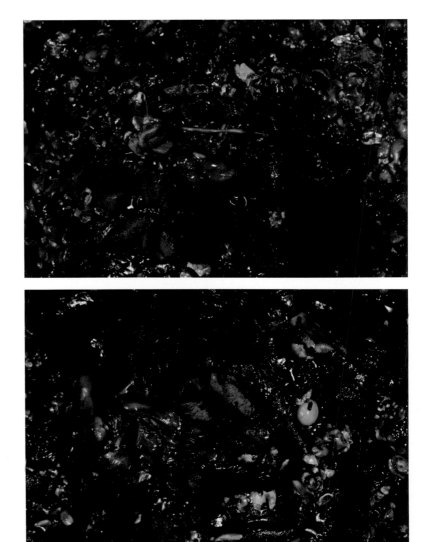

Untitled #190, 1989 (two panels)

Jay Shaun: There's food and slime all over. Did she use melted chocolate or gravy? I can see all kinds of fake body parts: a nose, a tongue, teeth, a mouth, eyeballs. It's gross. Art should look good so people can like it.

Chapter 5

The Next Really Big Thing

"I would go to a Salvation Army store and look for certain kinds of costume-y things. But so much of it was junky stuff. I would rip up a pair of pants and use the legs as sleeves for some other kind of garment that looked like brocade from the seventeenth century. But it was just some cut-up pieces of fabric."

History Pictures 1988–1990

The United States. France. Germany. Austria. New Zealand. Japan. By the late eighties, Cindy's artwork had been featured in dozens of countries in exhibitions at museums and galleries. With fame came offers that she could once only dream about. For Cindy, a grant for two months in Italy, all expenses paid, turned up at the right moment. It was time for an adventure.

She had already started a new group of artworks based on Old Master paintings. Now in Rome, around every corner she could find a church, museum, or public building filled with masterpieces. Those did not inspire her. Instead, she covered the walls of her studio with pages from art history books.

Untitled #193, 1989

Untitled #210, 1989

Sean (age 11): The man looks like he works for a church. His scarf has crosses on it and he's holding a cup of wine or holy water. He has a suspicious look on his face. It was a long time ago. There was no electricity. So a candle lights up the dark room. This reminds me of that movie *The Exorcist*. He's waiting to do an exorcism.

"It's an aspect of photography I appreciate," she says, "the idea that images can be seen and reproduced anywhere, by anyone."

She scoured flea markets for props. She draped herself in mostly cheap fabrics that, seen through the camera's lens, appeared to be luxurious. However, the use of false body parts—bulging bellies, breasts, huge noses, warts, beards, and giant feet—gave her large, flat photographs, complete with gilded frames, a faintly mocking quality.

Cindy says, "I don't think anybody even realizes that on the bottom right corner [of Untitled #193—seen on page 39] are these big toes on a huge foot. I thought, 'What if she's this beautiful, powdered, wigged woman but then she's got these big feet sticking out?'"

In most of Cindy's photographs, the subjects are female. But in History Portraits Cindy takes on the roles of several convincing male figures.

What is identity?

Would you ever guess that the prettily dressed woman on page 39 (Untitled #193) and the stern bearded man (Untitled #210) are the same person?

Do clothes and hairstyles make us what we are?

Faces in profile against a black background were a staple of sixteenth-century artwork—and so were imposing noses. Cindy's artwork of a hooded figure reminds us of such a painting.

The seam of the exaggerated fake nose is clearly visible. Here Cindy is enjoying herself, letting the viewer in on the joke.

Emperor Maxmilian I *by Ambrogio de Predis, 1502, oil on oak panel*

Untitled #219, 1990

Caravaggio's Young Sick Bacchus, *c. 1593, oil on canvas*

Untitled #224, 1990

Bacchus, who is the Roman god of wine and revelry, was painted in 1593 by the Italian painter Caravaggio. It is considered his self-portrait. The painting is nicknamed "Sick Bacchus" because of the yellowish skin tone. Caravaggio might have been suffering from a disease known as malaria. Cindy wasn't trying to copy Old Master paintings. How is the painting on the right different from the original?

Ananya: Bacchus is the god of wine. You can tell the artist didn't make herself up to be exactly the same as the famous painting. Her face looks more pinched, feminine.

Lilliana: The tables are different colors and Cindy has more grapes. Her crown is made of ivy leaves. And there are no peaches.

Clowns 2003–2004

On September 11, 2001, a group of terrorists hijacked four American airplanes. They crashed two into the twin towers of the World Trade Center in New York City. Another smashed into the Pentagon building in Washington, D.C. The fourth plummeted into a field in Pennsylvania after

Untitled #424, 2004

brave passengers fought back. For many Americans the world changed that day.

"I'd been going through a struggle, particularly after 9/11," says Cindy. "I couldn't figure out what I wanted to say. I still wanted the work to be the same kind of mixture—intense, with a nasty side or an ugly side, but also with a real pathos about the characters—and [clowns] have an underlying sense of sadness while they're trying to cheer people up."

One of her biggest challenges was disguising her face under the makeup, "so it wouldn't seem like they were just me with clown makeup on." She discarded photographs she thought looked too much like her. For the first time, Cindy used Photoshop to create the swirling backgrounds.

Karl: I think there's something wrong with these clowns. The eyes, the huge mouth, the clothes, all look creepy. The male might be saying to the female, "What's wrong with you? Have you looked in the mirror lately?" They must not be working. If they were, they'd look happier to make kids smile.

Gunnar: The expression on her face is like, "I'm going to eat you, children." The other clown with the blank face might be terrified by the clown next to him.

Untitled #420, 2004 (two panels)

Society Pictures 2008

Before Cindy had even thought about being an artist, she'd dressed up in her great-grandmother's clothes and pretended to be old. Now as a successful artist for almost thirty years, she saw aging from another point of view. The portraits in this series are of overly groomed high-society types, wives of the rich and famous.

"It's a little scary when I see myself. It's especially scary when I see myself in these older women."

After posing in her studio wearing a long, sumptuous caftan, Cindy digitally added an elegant setting that she had shot at the Cloisters, a museum in New York City.

The artist might have put on those plastic shoes and support hose to signify the reality of growing older. Yet this also adds humor to such a self-important pose.

Untitled #468, 2008

Lexie: She looks proper, like my grandmother. She would wear a long dress like that, flowing, an elegant older lady, but not those shoes. The shoes look like hospital shoes, like she needs an operation on her feet.

Lucy: That's not her real hair color. She looks like a Coco Chanel type—jacket, gloves, and scarf—but older, unhappy. Rich. She's waiting for someone who is late. She isn't patient, she's annoyed. I don't think I'd like her.

Untitled #466, 2008

Chapter 6

Looking Backward, Looking Forward

"None of the characters are me. They're everything but me. If it seems too close to me, it's rejected."

February 2012. New York City. The Museum of Modern Art (MoMA)

Collectors, artists, curators, movie stars, and fashionistas swarmed the sixth-floor galleries to celebrate Cindy's work. For an American artist, an exhibit at MoMA is like winning the Super Bowl or an Academy Award.

When people stepped off the elevator, they were confronted with five oddly garbed, eighteen-foot-tall women looming against a grainy black-and-off-white landscape.

The woodsy background was shot by the artist in New York's Central Park. Cindy reworked this setting in Photoshop to look

Museum of Modern Art, 2012

Untitled #548, 2010/2012

like drawings. The huge murals were printed on high-quality contact paper that sticks to the wall.

Notice the faces of the women. They lack Cindy's usual painstaking process of adding on layers of cosmetics and body parts. She says, "I didn't use any makeup . . . But then I started changing the faces digitally to slightly alter them, so it's kind of like using Photoshop instead of makeup."

"It's horrifying how easy it is to make changes," she admits.

Past these peculiar sentinels and through the museum, the history of Cindy's work filled the galleries. From room to room, a hundred seventy-one pictures peered out from the walls—an unfolding cast of her characters: a bored housewife, a young hitchhiker, a tough biker, a startled clown.

From her early college artworks and the first small Untitled Film Stills to these large murals, Cindy has consistently changed and grown. It takes courage for an artist who achieves success not to stay with what works, but instead to try something new and unpredictable.

An exhibit like this, drawn from every period of an artist's career, is called a retrospective. It can feel like a summing-up of a life's work. Yet while the MoMA exhibit was still wowing the public, Cindy began showing a new, risky group of large-scale color photographs downtown at Metro Pictures. They served notice that Cindy was still challenging herself.

The harsh and moody backgrounds were photographed by Cindy in Iceland. Her characters are so theatrically placed against the barren ridge that they could be from another planet. Cindy's fascination with fashion is evident in their vintage Chanel costumes. But again she distorts our notions about a usual fashion layout. Who are these people? As always, the artist leaves the story up to us.

Five years after her MoMA triumph, Cindy unveiled a new set of large-scale portraits. In these she adopts the role of aging movie stars from Hollywood's golden age. Cindy says,

"They are the most sincere things I've done—that aren't full of irony or caricature or cartoonishness—since Film Stills."

The women in this series pose in costumes they once wore as starlets, some in negligees, others in more elaborate fashions.

Untitled #579, 2016

In Untitled #579, a former screen siren with a pouty, come-hither expression twirls her hair and puckers her lips in a girlish pose. Despite her makeup and long, curly tresses, we see she is no longer young.

As the artist faces growing older, so do her subjects. Unlike Cindy's portraits of mature women in the past, these once-famous beauties might look vulnerable, but they are also strong, self-confident, looking forward to what comes next.

We've seen hundreds of photographs of Cindy, but where is she? Would we recognize her? Again and again articles about the artist have asked, "Will the real Cindy Sherman please stand up?"

Now we realize that the real Cindy Sherman has been standing up all along. She might change her body or her face, change herself from one character to another, yet from the very beginning of her work she's been telling us to look at what she sees, how she views the world, what she thinks. There are many facets and faces of the real Cindy Sherman.

A beauty. A clown. An aging movie star. An outsider. An insider.

When we look at Cindy's personas, we can't help but think of ourselves. The figures don't exist in a vacuum.

They are about her.
They are about us.

Cindy at the MoMA opening, 2012 (opposite)

Untitled #571, 2016

Production Notes

Looking at Untitled #571, 2016

This is from Cindy Sherman's 2016 series of screen stars. We know that the artist uses a camera to photograph herself in many roles. What part is she playing in this picture? At first glance we see a woman in a red-and-white-striped caftan draped on a shearling throw. Behind her is a woodsy scene of a lake and trees at dusk. She is dressed elegantly in a turban and long gown. Let's look at the parts of this artwork, pull it apart, and put it back together again.

Color: Our eyes are drawn to the central image, the woman in a silvery turban, her pale face highlighted by dark branches.

Texture: Her gown is silky, glossy, in contrast to the thick, shaggy fur coverlet.

Line: The stripes on the gown are a familiar pattern, like the American flag, a circus tent, or a popular summer T-shirt.

Shape: The large figure dominates the picture. She is definitely center stage.

Focus: The blurred background of the lake and trees looks like a fake backdrop. We know this is a photograph. The setting is inserted digitally. The sharp focus of the figure separates her from the landscape. We can almost pluck her out of the picture.

What is the feeling expressed in this portrait? Here are some adjectives to describe the mood: *Dreamy. Thoughtful. Satisfied. Poised. Confident. Successful.* The woman holds our gaze. Her face is turned away, her mouth curved in a half smile. Notice her hand fingering her necklace in a coy way. Is she looking at someone else in the room? Or is she lost in thought? Dressed as the starlet she once was, she now is a mature woman, posing for the camera one more time.

Facts about Cindy You May Not Know

- She bicycles around New York City.

- She loves to shop.

- She illustrated a children's book, *Fitcher's Bird* by the Brothers Grimm.

- She used to surf in the ocean near her house in Long Island, New York.

- She wrote and directed a movie called *Office Killer* with Hollywood stars.

- She had a cameo role in John Waters's film *Pecker*.

- She was the first woman artist in the world to sell a photograph for $1,000,000.

- She won a MacArthur Fellowship, a $500,000 award to encourage her work.

- She was married to French filmmaker Michel Auder from 1984 to 1999.

- She lives in a loft in downtown New York with her pet bird, a twenty-five-year-old macaw.

- She has had more than seventy-five solo exhibitions and over 150 group exhibitions of her work in the United States and all over the world.

Cindy Sherman, Untitled #E57 (Art News *cover), 1983*

Cindy Sherman's Process and Practice in Her Own Words

While Cindy might have an idea of what she wants to express, she says if she knew how her work would come out beforehand she wouldn't do it. She likes surprising herself.

The child Cindy dressed up to fool the neighbors, to playact with her friends. For the grown-up Cindy, dressing up is one of the steps in her art-making process. Her transformation into a role is long, intense, and private. In the mirror she sees an angle or an expression that catches her imagination. "Suddenly the reflection I'm looking at is not at all me. Suddenly it's like a phantom that's just popped out of the mirror, and that's when I know the character is right on."

"There have been moments where I remember this thing suddenly appearing and I can't believe that's me!"

Taking photographs is another step, the one that records the transformation. She moves around to get different poses and camera angles.

When she looks at the exposures on the computer, she might find an unexpected image. That might be the one that works best.

While she develops a character with makeup and clothing, she listens to music. "I can't work without it," says Cindy. "And it has to be the right kind, because if it's not then I get into a bad mood. I work with a remote so that I can change music instantly if I need to."

With the Clown series in 2004, Cindy began to use Photoshop for the backgrounds of her photographs. In 2007 she started shooting both the backgrounds and the figures digitally. "Now that I'm working digitally, I have everything hooked up to my computer, so I just take ten shots, and go see how the focus is. And what it means is that once I start working, I figure, 'OK, I'm all made up, I might as well just keep working.' "

For her more recent series in 2016, the artist used a new process in which photographic dyes are transferred directly onto aluminum instead of onto paper. The Metal Print is scratch resistant, so the need for glass protection is eliminated. The surface has a glow that, along with the large size of the picture, brings the figure to life.

Photography is Cindy's medium in the same way that another artist might use paint and canvas. Painting has been classified as "fine art" since the seventeenth century. Although early camera photography, invented in the nineteenth century, originally was used to document real events, people, or places, it has quickly evolved into its own distinct art form. Cindy Sherman is credited with being the most important artist to blur the lines between these separate artistic worlds.

Interior of Cindy Sherman's studio
filled with props, 2012

Bibliography

Detail from Untitled #92

Books

Cruz, Amana, and A. T. Elizabeth Smith. *Cindy Sherman Retrospective*. Chicago: Thames & Hudson, 1997. In conjunction with the exhibition organized by the Museum of Contemporary Art, Los Angeles, and the Museum of Contemporary Art, Chicago.

Danto, Arthur C. *Cindy Sherman: History Portraits*. New York: Rizzoli International Publications, 1991.

Durand, Régis, Jean-Pierre Criqui, and Laura Mulvey. *Cindy Sherman*. Paris: Flammarion–Jeu de Paume, 2006.

Galassi, Peter, and Cindy Sherman. *Cindy Sherman: The Complete Untitled Film Stills*. New York: Museum of Modern Art, 2003.

Moorhouse, Paul. *Cindy Sherman*. New York and London: Phaidon Focus–Phaidon Press Ltd., 2014.

Morris, Catherine. *The Essential Cindy Sherman*. New York: Harry N. Abrams, Inc., 1999.

Respini, Eva, Johanna Burton, and John Waters. *Cindy Sherman*. New York: Museum of Modern Art, 2012.

Schjeldahl, Peter, and Lisa Philips. *Cindy Sherman*. New York: The Whitney Museum of Contemporary Art, 1987.

Schor, Gabriele. *Cindy Sherman: The Early Works 1975-77*. Catalogue Raisonne. Vienna: HatjeCantz; New York: Metro Pictures, 2012.

Articles

Baker, Kenneth. "Cindy Sherman Show at SFMOMA Opens." *San Francisco Chronicle*, July 8, 2012. www.sfgate.com/art/article/Cindy-Sherman-show-at-SFMOMA-opens-3686397.php.

Frankel, David. "Cindy Sherman Talks to David Frankel ('80s Then)." *Artforum International* 41, no. 7 (March 2003), pp. 54–55, 259–60.

Fuku, Noriko. "Cindy Sherman: A Woman of Parts." *Art in America*, January 1997, pp. 74–81, 125.

Glasscock, Jessica. Untitled article on a series of photos for Comme des Garçons. lurvemag.tumblr.com/post/243652242/in-1994-cindy-sherman-produced-a-series-of.

Gopnik, Blake. "Ready for Her Close-Up." *New York Times*, April 21, 2016. Arts and Leisure section, pp, 1, 18.

Hattenstone, Simon. "Cindy Sherman: Me, Myself and I." *The Guardian*, January 14, 2011. Weekend section, pp. 1, 12.

Herriman, Kat, and Gay Gassmann. "Match the Artist with Their Childhood Works, Round 2." *New York Times Magazine*, September 10, 2015.

Hoban, Phoebe. "The Cindy Sherman Effect." *Art News*, February 14, 2012. www.artnews.com/2012/02/14/the-cindy-sherman-effect.

Lichtenstein, Therese. Interview with Cindy Sherman. *Journal of Contemporary Art*, 1997. www.jca-online.com/sherman.html.

Museum of Modern Art. "Major Series of Photographs by Cindy Sherman Acquired by the Museum of Modern Art." Press release, January 18, 1996.

Sischy, Ingrid. "Cindy Sherman: The Artist's Studio." *Vanity Fair*. March 2012. www.vanityfair.com/culture/2012/03/cindy-sherman-moma-201203.

Stevens, Mark. "How I Made It: Cindy Sherman on Her 'Untitled Film Stills.'" *New York*, April 7, 2008. nymag.com/anniversary/40th/culture/45773.

Tomkins, Calvin. "Her Secret Identities." *The New Yorker*, May 15, 2000, pp. 78–79.

Vogel, Carol. "Cindy Sherman Unmasked." *New York Times*, February 16, 2012. www.nytimes.com/2012/02/19/arts/design/moma-to-showcase-cindy-shermans-new-and-old-characters.html.

Websites

www.cindysherman.com/biography.shtml. A private tribute website not associated with Cindy Sherman or her representatives.

www.moma.org/interactives/exhibitions/2012/cindysherman/gallery/video. "My Favorite Cindy Sherman." Filmed interviews with ten art-world notables including Robert Longo and Helene Winer.

www.tate.org.uk/context-comment/articles/studio-cindy-sherman. The website for the Tate Museums in the UK.

Video

"Nobody's Here but Me." www.youtube.com/watch?v=UXKNuWtXZ_U. 1994. A fifty-five-minute video about Cindy Sherman's art practice produced by the BBC.

Office Killer, DVD. Directed by Cindy Sherman. Dimension Home Video, 2002.

Portrait of an Artist at Work: Cindy Sherman. Directed by Michel Auder. Michel Auder Videos, 1988. Videocassette.

Notes

Detail from Untitled #210

All unattributed quotes are from Cindy Sherman directly to the authors.

Meet Cindy Sherman

6 "I would make myself . . .": Respini, p. 14.

9 "trying to trick . . .": Schor, p. 14.

Chapter 1 Where It All Began

11 "There were no sidewalks . . .": Schor, p. 13.

11 Cindy received . . . : Schor, p. 13.

12 *I Love Lucy,* 1951–1960, America's most popular TV show, starring Lucille Ball and her then-husband Desi Arnaz. It has been in reruns ever since.

12 "I was the youngest . . .": Schor, p. 13.

12 "The beach was rocky . . .": Schor, p. 12.

13 "I was always the kid . . .": Schjeldahl, p. 19.

13 "I'd put on makeup every day of the year . . .": Hattenstone.

13 "My idea of being an artist . . .": www .cindysherman.com/biography.shtml.

13 caption: "When I was in high school . . .": Herriman.

Chapter 2 College Days

14 "I always felt like an artist . . .": Schor, p. 15.

14 "Home was not home . . .": Schor, p. 16.

15 "None of that . . .": Fuku, p. 75.

15 Barbara Jo Revelle is a photographer, film/video maker, and installation and public artist. She is now a professor and the director of the Photography Area at the University of Florida, Gainesville.

15 "strangely dazzling . . .": Schor, p. 18.

15 "not being serious": Schor, p. 18.

15 "I was demoted from . . .": A bachelor of fine arts is a more prestigious college degree than a bachelor of arts, which is what Cindy was granted. Schor, p. 18.

15 "did not wear makeup . . .": Hattenstone.

17 Robert Longo (b. 1953 in Brooklyn, New York) is an American painter and sculptor.

18 "I decided to use the camera . . .": Schor, p. 11.

19 The National Endowment for the Arts is a federal program supporting the arts.

19 "You've got the money . . .": walkerart .org (Robert Longo).

Chapter 3 New York, New York

20 "I didn't think I was actually going to make a difference . . .": Frankel.

20 At that time Fulton Street was a commercial area of New York. An open-air wholesale fish market was located there from 1822 until 2005.

20 "I liked her . . .": MoMA.org (Helene Winer).

20 "I'd be home . . .": Sischy.

21 "If you look at one . . .": Stevens.

21 "I wanted them to . . .": Tomkins.

22 "I took a couple . . .": Galassi, p. 16.

22 "She looked pretty . . .": MoMA.org (Robert Longo).

25 "I like the idea . . .": Photoquotations.

25 "a landmark body . . .": Museum of Modern Art.

Chapter 4 Rear Screen Projections, Centerfolds, Fairy Tales, and More

27 "When I'm working . . .": Tomkins.

27 "Black-and-white lends . . .": Fuku.

28 "I wanted to comment . . .": Respini, p. 78.

29 "Even though I've . . .": Fuku.

31 "Briefly in the '80s . . .": Respini, p. 68.

33 "I grew up . . .": Lichtenstein.

33 "I'm disgusted . . .": Respini, pp. 32–33.

33 "Once I'm set up . . .": Morris, p. 16.

37 "It intrigues me why certain . . .": Lichtenstein.

Chapter 5 The Next Really Big Thing

38 "I would go to a Salvation . . .": Respini, p. 75.

41 "It's an aspect of . . .": Respini, p. 43.

41 "I don't think anybody . . .": Lichtenstein.

41 Giovanni Ambrogio de Predis (c.1455–1508), an Italian painter who worked with Leonardo da Vinci.

42 Michelangelo Merisi da Caravaggio (1571–1610), an Italian artist famous for his dramatic use of light and shadow (called chiaroscuro).

42 Malaria is a disease carried by mosquitoes. In serious cases the victim can develop yellow skin.

44 "I'd been going through . . .": Hattenstone.

44 "so it wouldn't seem . . .": Baker.

46 "It's a little scary . . .": Tomkins.

46 Coco Chanel was a famous French fashion designer (1883–1971). We asked Lucy how she knew about her and she replied, "I saw a movie on TV."

Chapter 6 Looking Backward, Looking Forward

48 "None of the characters . . .": Vogel.

50 "I didn't use any . . .": Respini, p. 79.

50 "It's horrifying . . .": Vogel.

51 "They are the most sincere . . .": Gopnik.

Cindy's Process and Practice

58 "Suddenly the reflection . . .": Sischy.

58 "There have been moments . . .": Sischy.

58 "I can't work without it . . .": Hattenstone.

58 "Now that I'm working . . .": Hoban.

List of Artworks by Cindy Sherman

Artworks by Cindy Sherman courtesy of the artist and Metro Pictures.

Most of the artist's series are in editions of six.

pp. 1, 54–55: Untitled #571, 2016. Dye sublimation metal print, 54 × 69½ inches.

p. 2: Untitled #415, 2004. Chromogenic color print, 68 × 44½ inches.

pp. 4–5: Untitled Film Still #13, 1978.

Detail from "A Cindy Book"

pp. 10–11: "A Cindy Book," ca. 1964–75. Paper and staples, 26 photographs on 14 pages.

p. 13: Untitled (Easy Rider).

pp. 14–15: Untitled, 1975. 23 black-and-white photographs in an accordion booklet, hand-colored.

p. 17: Untitled (Lucy), 1975/2001. Gelatin silver print.

p. 18: *Doll Clothes*, 1975. 16-mm film, black-and-white, silent.

p. 18–19: Scale Relationship Series (Version II), 1976. 37 black-and-white cutout photographs mounted on board.

p. 19: Installation view with various cutouts by Sherman in the backseat of her car, Snow Show, Hallwalls Contemporary Art Center, February 1977.

Detail from Untitled (Secretary)

p. 21: *Untitled (Secretary)*, Cindy at Artists Space, 1978/1993. Gelatin silver print.

p. 22: Murder Mystery, 1976. 4 of 255 black-and-white cutout photographs.

pp. 22–23: Untitled Film Still #25, 1978. Gelatin silver print, 7 9/16 × 9½ inches.

p. 24: Untitled Film Still #48, 1979. Gelatin silver print, 7 7/16 × 9 7/16 inches.

Detail from Untitled #66

p. 26: Untitled #66, 1980. Chromogenic color print, 16 × 23 15/16 inches.

p. 28: Untitled #96, 1981. Chromogenic color print, 24 × 48 inches.

p. 29: Untitled #92, 1981. Chromogenic color print, 24 × 48 inches.

pp. 30–31: Untitled #90, 1981. Chromogenic color print, 24 × 48 inches.

p. 32: Untitled #122, 1983. Chromogenic color print, 75¾ × 45¾ inches.

Detail from Untitled #119

p. 33: Untitled #119, 1983. Chromogenic color print, 48½ × 94 inches.

p. 34: Untitled #150, 1985. Chromogenic color print, 49½ × 66¾ inches.

p. 35: Untitled #153, 1985. Chromogenic color print, 67¼ × 49½ inches.

p. 36: Untitled #172, 1987. Photograph, Edition 6 of 6, 71½ × 47½ inches.

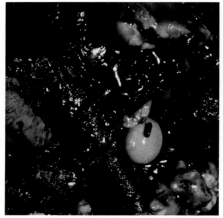

Detail from Untitled #190

p. 37: Untitled #190, 1989. Two chromogenic color prints, 48¼ × 73 inches each.

p. 39: Untitled #193, 1989. Chromogenic color print, 48⁷/₈ × 41¹⁵/₁₆ inches.

p. 40: Untitled #210, 1989. Chromogenic color print, 66 × 44 inches.

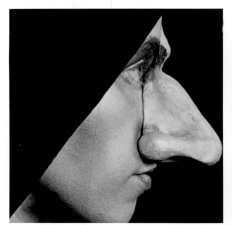

Detail from Untitled #219

p. 41: Untitled #219, 1990. Chromogenic color print, 65 × 40 inches.

p. 42: Untitled #224, 1990. Chromogenic color print, 48 × 38 inches.

p. 43: Untitled #424, 2004. Chromogenic color print, 53³/₄ × 54³/₄ inches.

Detail from Untitled #420

pp. 44–45: Untitled #420, 2004. Two chromogenic color prints, 71¹³/₁₆ × 45⁵/₈ inches each.

p. 46: Untitled #468, 2008. Chromogenic color print, 70¹/₄ × 54 inches.

p. 47: Untitled #466, 2008. Chromogenic color print, 96 × 70 inches.

pp. 50–51: Untitled #548, 2010/2012. Chromogenic color print, 70¹/₂ × 139 inches.

p. 52: Untitled #579, 2016. Dye sublimation metal print, 58¹/₂ × 46³/₄ inches.

Detail from Untitled #571

pp. 54–55, Untitled #571, 2016. Dye sublimation metal print, 54 × 69¹/₂ inches.

Detail from Untitled #E57

p. 57: Untitled #E57 (cover of *Art News*), 1983. Chromogenic color print, 15¹/₄ × 10¹/₂ inches.

Photography Credits

The authors gratefully acknowledge the permissions granted to reproduce the copyrighted material in this book. Photographs not otherwise credited are courtesy of Cindy Sherman and Metro Pictures.

Photograph of Cindy and her friend Janet (p. 7), courtesy of Cindy Sherman and Metro Pictures.

Photograph of Museum of Modern Art banner (pp. 8–9), LHB Photo Alamy.

Photograph of Lucille Ball from *I Love Lucy* (p. 12, left), Everett Collection.

Photograph of interior of thrift store (p. 12, right), New York City/Alamy.

Photographs of Ashford Hollow Foundation (p. 16), courtesy of Cindy Sherman and Metro Pictures.

Photograph of Fulton Street sign (p. 21), Dirk Kaufman.

Photograph of Museum of Modern Art (pp. 48–49), courtesy of Cindy Sherman and Metro Pictures.

Photograph of Cindy Sherman at the MoMA opening (p. 53), Getty Images.

Photograph of the interior of Cindy Sherman's studio (p. 59), courtesy of Martyn Thompson.

Acknowledgments

Many people worked with us to make this book possible. Our most profound thanks go to the artist Cindy Sherman, the star of and inspiration for this book. We appreciate the help of the staff at her gallery, Metro Pictures: the well-informed and obliging registrars Michael Plunkett and Pericles Kolias and the always gracious director, Tom Heman. Thanks also go to Jeanne Greenberg Rohatyn, who introduced us to Cindy Sherman; our energetic and enthusiastic agent, Laurie Liss; our good friend and editor, Neal Porter, whose advice and guidance have been invaluable for many years; supportive and caring assistant editor Emily Feinberg; always helpful managing editor Jill Freshney; thorough copy editor Karla Reganold; and attentive production manager Susan Doran. Thanks also to our affable and creative designer, Dirk Kaufman. A special thanks to Dolores B. Malcolm, director of RIF (Reading Is Fundamental) in St. Louis, who organized our visits to talk to fifth graders in the St. Louis Public Schools. To Tuan Nguyen, director of education, and Lisa Melandri, director of the Contemporary Art Museum of St. Louis, thank you for introducing us to the students participating in LEAP, your middle school art program. Last but definitely not least, a big thank-you to our thirteen delightful young people who joined us from New York, St. Louis, and Boulder to talk about Cindy Sherman's artworks: Ananya, Arianna, Coco, Frankie, Gunnar, Jay Shaun, Karl, Kit, Lexie, Lilliana, Lucy, Madeline, and Sean.